The Mystic of Sex

ANAÏS NIN

The Mystic of Sex
AND OTHER WRITINGS

Edited and with a Preface by Gunther Stuhlmann

CAPRA PRESS
SANTA BARBARA

Library of Congress Cataloging-in-Publication Data
Nin, Anaïs, 1903-1977
The mystic of sex : a first look at D.H. Lawrence uncollected
writings, 1931-1974 / Anaïs Nin.
p. cm.
ISBN 0-88496-391-8
1. Nin, Anaïs, 1903-1977—Aesthetics. 2. Lawrence, D.H.
(David Herbert), 1885-1930—Criticism and interpretation.
3. Sex in literature. I. Title
PS3527.I865A6 1995   95-2129
814'.52—dc20   CIP

CAPRA PRESS
P.O. Box 2068, Santa Barbara, CA 93120

CONTENTS

PREFACE

"Why one writes is a question I can answer easily, having so often asked it of myself," Anaïs Nin told an audience in 1971 when, in the wake of the publication of the first volumes of her *Diary*, she was at the zenith of her lecturing career before illness forced her to abandon all public appearances. "I believe one writes because one has to create a world in which one can live. I could not live in any of the worlds offered to me—the world of my parents, the world of war, the world of politics. I had to create a world of my own, like a climate, a country, an atmosphere in which I could breathe, reign, and recreate myself when destroyed by living. That, I believe, is the reason for every work of art."

Anaïs Nin's major work of art, of course, was the enormous diary she began in 1914, at the age of eleven, and faithfully kept as her only reliable companion until her death early in 1977, a few weeks short of her seventy-fourth birthday. Yet for many years, until she was in her sixties, these

diaries—more than 35,000 pages—defied all efforts at publication, for personal and practical reasons, and Anaïs Nin,
the writer, became known only for the fictions she distilled
from this highly charged, self-probing emotional material.
"What is it allotted me to say?" she had written in her first
book of fiction, *The House of Incest*, in 1936, "Only the truth
disguised as a fairy tale, and this is the fairy tale behind
which all the truths are staring as behind grilled mosque
windows."

Anaïs Nin eventually found a way to prepare and release
some of her lifelong artistic endeavor, at first in an edited
form which eliminated the still private aspects of her life as
a sensuous, sexual woman. Today, there are in print thirteen
volumes drawn from the original diary pages. We have the
complete, unabridged four volumes of *The Early Diary of
Anaïs Nin* for the years 1914 to 1931, which cover her adoles-
cence in "exile" in America, the courtship of and idealistic
marriage to Hugh Guiler, her "banker-poet," and the emerg-
ing unrest of her sexual awakening while living in France
(which found its first public expression, perhaps, in her
first—albeit pseudonymous—publication in 1930, her essay
on D.H. Lawrence, "The Mystic of Sex," reproduced in these
pages). We have the seven edited volumes of *The Diary of
Anaïs Nin*, which began to appear in 1966, presenting what
could be told at the time about her life as an artist and the

world she created for herself and others between 1932 and 1974. And with the ongoing publication of *A Journal of Love*, freed by her own death and that of her husband in 1985 from the protective prohibitions she had once imposed upon herself—and rescinded in her last will and testament—we now have the missing parts which complete the unvarnished, often wrenching, often contradictory "self-portrait" Anaïs Nin had wanted us to have when all of her "private" diary could be published.

The writings collected in this volume—except for a few small, personal diary excerpts—are expressions of the "public" writer Anaïs Nin. They span a period of more than forty years. They bring together, for the first time, Anaïs Nin's combative pamphlets and essays of the 1940s and 1950s, when she felt neglected and ostracized by the American literary establishment, dismissed as a "surrealist," an avant-garde writer of psychoanalytical "case histories," when the distillations of emotional truth and Proustian analysis from her diaries, these explorations of an inner world, found no echo among what she called "the reporters and realists," the politically engaged, who then dominated American literary life. But Anaïs Nin set out not only to defend her own way of writing, she also wanted to advocate new approaches, a new sensibility in literature, born of her own artistic struggles, which eventually culminated in the volume, *The*

Novel of the Future, published in 1968. "The richest source of creation is feeling," she wrote, "followed by a vision of its meaning. The medium of the writer is not ink and paper but his body, the sensitivity of his eyes, ears, and heart. If they are atrophied, let him give up writing."

Some of the writing here collected appeared for the first time, or was rediscovered and republished, in the pages of *ANAÏS: An International Journal*, the annual I created and have edited since 1982, under the sponsorship of the Nin Foundation and the Nin Trust, under its Trustee, Rupert Pole, who also made this volume possible. The enormous response to the initial publication of *The Diary of Anaïs Nin* in the 1960s, of course, brought her numerous invitations to preface and introduce books by other writers, to lecture, to comment on the "new woman" Anaïs herself represented to so many of her readers. On all these occasions Anaïs Nin inevitably continued, as the items here collected show, to advocate and promote the kind of creative literary climate she herself had worked so hard to achieve, both in her diary and in her "public" writing. Yet, unlike so many others who become convinced of the rightness of their ideas, Anaïs Nin always seems to have remembered what she had so forcefully expressed, when she was twenty-eight years old, in her first published essay on D.H. Lawrence:

"Poetry and the bare truth exist side by side. Pity wavers back and forth, just as ideas do, and convictions. Lawrence knew there was no finality, no solution, no ground one could be certain never to want to move away from. If you are terribly truthful the ground will always move from under you, you will have to shift with shifting truth. You will crave a definite idea (that is our hell), you may worship one, but you will also shift with shifting truth, just as Lawrence did."

Gunther Stuhlmann
Becket, Massachusetts
spring 1994

THE MYSTIC OF SEX—
A first look at D.H. Lawrence

D.H. LAWRENCE has been difficult to measure because he is the kind of writer who rouses either enthusiasm or hate. No one can hold a neutral opinion of him; he is too definite a personality, and the world he created in his books is too vigorous and unique to be overlooked.

Lawrence the poet, passionately truthful, angered the moralists. Lawrence the propagandist distressed the poets. In judging him people were either drawn to or repelled by his philosophy.

There is no doubt that Lawrence had an active philosophy and that he wished to convert others to it. But it was not a mere idea, a coolly constructed formula he wished to impose. He was, like all true poets, against tepid living and tepid loves. He resented the lack of feeling in people, or what is worse, the lack of expression of such feelings; he wanted a fulfillment of physical life equal to the mental; he wanted to reawaken impulse, and the clairvoyance of our intuitions. All this in him overflowed with rich intensity, an intensity which was understood by the lyrically minded—the poets— and by the moderns who approve excess for the sake of uncompromising frankness. But the rest considered him an outcast. They were made uneasy by his ever-questioning characters, by the obscurity and struggles of their minds, by the uncanny discoveries reached by Lawrence's application of intuitional reasoning.

Lawrence's naturalness would not seem exaggerated to the Latin mind; in fact, to the Latin mind he is essentially a mystic. This is not a paradox. Lawrence's physically-rooted philosophy has obscured the fact of his mysticism. We find this mysticism in the most physical of all his books: *Lady Chatterley's Lover*. In this book it is the sexual relation between man and woman almost exclusively which is described, yet Lawrence clearly indicates the way through the physical into the feeling of love. From an artistic point of view it is his most unbalanced book, and humanly, his most incomplete one, because he considers no other relationship but the sexual one. But he has done so in such a way that his description of the sexual passion surpasses all that has ever been written on the subject, not only in physical plenitude, but also in deep emotional completeness. Lawrence wrote neither scientifically, nor for the sake of pornography. He wrote as a poet, not obsessed with sex, but so sensitive to it that he could make all kinds of subtle distinctions about it. No one who is enslaved by sex can make such distinctions; they can only be made by a clear mind and a rich imagination. Lawrence not only gave full expression to the gestures of passion, but—and that is what most people failed to see— he indicated precisely those feelings surrounding sexual experience, and springing from it, which make passion a consummation both of our human and of our imaginative life. Lawrence's man, Mellors, had passed through sex into love— the ideal. He had known other kinds of desire and discarded them. Desire, when selective, ceases to be obscene. Lawrence then places in the center of this physical intensity that strangely delicate rarity: tenderness—which ordinary sexuality never makes room for; which has never appeared in other books at the same time as ordinary sexuality, and which is specially absent in Latin literature, so adept in the description of passion. Here is Lawrence the poet and mystic—uncovering the very mystery of true passion, which is half mystical. When there is tenderness, and selection (Lady Chatterley and Mellors chose each other deliberately because together they could reach absolute livingness), when there is the sense of individuality, of completeness, there is no longer just sex. Yet Lawrence is an outcast because his feelings take root from the flesh.

In this book there are ugly words—strong, crude, ugly. But to anyone familiar with Lawrence's writing it is evident that they were used defiantly, as a challenge to timorous, squeamish people. Lawrence felt that an honest facing of them, a natural use of them, might deprive them of their ugliness and change their meaning. He wrote: "When it comes to the meaning of anything, even the simplest word, then you must pause. Because there are two great categories of meaning, forever separate. There is mob-meaning and there is individual meaning." He asks us to take the individual meaning. He makes us directly responsible for the interpretation of words. The fact that he has taken certain words which are ugly and used them simply as if they were strong, powerful, expressive, natural, and that they remain ugly, proves that the old, familiar connotation, the general one, is stronger and almost impossible to change. "The word will take the individual off on his own journey, and its meaning will be his own meaning, based on his own genuine imaginative reaction. And when a word comes to us in its individual character, and starts in us the individual responses, it is a great pleasure to us." Lawrence gives us that pleasure continuously, all through his books. The individualists understand him. Other people think he was a mere anarchist. And at certain exasperated moments he was. Some of his reactions were excessive. He was unhinged by bitterness. A great deal of rebellious, combative thinking misses ultimate truth. Great writers have generally found themselves only when they freed themselves of their antagonisms. But Lawrence was never free, and he found himself because he was strong enough to create poetry out of his antagonisms, his anger, his bitterness, his solitariness. And he did more than that; he described perfectly two sides of life; the sexual, and the mystical.

It is in this way that he was balanced. Balance is a philosophic ideal, not a human state. Lawrence was sensuous; he worked with and through feeling. He had therefore the divination of physical love to its fullest measure, and also perception into a second world. Precisely because he was a physical man, a man who felt words and their meaning with his five senses, he was better able to lead us into that world completely, without getting lost in abstract vagaries. He had the true double vision; he saw divinity of spirit wherever it was, not where it should be. Now it appeared in a horse (*St. Mawr*) who was heroic and untrammeled, now in the Australian bush, where a youth finds an intelligent god; now in savages; often in the body of man or woman.

He made room for the improbable. He was conscious of differences—another mark of the poet. He had no fear of disturbing his story when a groom feels like talking suddenly about fairies (*St. Mawr*), no fear of upsetting all scientific deductions about human nature to take us back to its darker, occult mysteries, into wonder again, deeper and deeper, into the puzzle of individuality, of personality, the unexpected tricks of our impulses, of our imagination, of our transformations, disintegration; and into the possibility of vision and understanding through our animal senses as well as through the mind. In a way he takes each man back to the beginning of the world, as if each man had to settle it all again for himself, begin his own world, find his god, obey obscure impulses which sometimes have their source in a second hidden nature within us which clear reason rarely reveals to our consciousness.

◆

Very often Lawrence would go off the track. Going off the track of consecutive thinking is a peculiar trick of the mystical mind. If it did not go off the track it would quietly stay on the main road forever saying A. leads to B. and B. to C. which is true, but very unexciting. Lawrence made it a practice to see what C. and A. together could explode or reveal. Logic and sequence are often poor guides to the seeker among shoreless seas, and pathless mountains, in which many an important truth has lain hidden.

This has been the special power of several English writers. There is in them a wise madness. Something in their mental life has taken its character from the English mists.

Mists make walls temporarily invisible. To many delightful imaginists walls have always been invisible. Lawrence was not among the delightful kind—rather he was dark and sombre—but he had that vision. Everything in his world is either alive or dead, always in the truest sense. Livingness was the first law. Livingness physically and imaginatively. Livingness in Lawrence included the power to resuscitate by feeling—(a miracle!) the power of renewal, always by feeling. To be alive in the real world through sex, and in the unreal through mysticism was to be completely alive. Who could say that Lawrence was unbalanced? He was acutely super-balanced.

Sometimes Lawrence's streak of disconnectedness leads nowhere, or as in "The Princess" it leads to a disappointment. The Princess, began mystically—there is no daintier, no more aloof Princess than she in literature—is suddenly transformed, in support of his sex theme, into an ordinary spinster who suffers from repression and cannot accept man as a whole. Here Lawrence, worried by the fact that sex had not been given its natural place in the Anglo-Saxon world, had to give it an unduly large one in a story. He could not wait and let the Princess grow up to a slow acceptance of love and passion. He did violence to her; he was angry with her.

The struggle which unbalances Lawrence at moments (and which worries the censors) is that between the physical and the mental.

See *Women in Love*. The outline is simple. Two sisters love two men of very different temperaments. One loves a man who is essentially a male, and a none too subtle one. Later, too late, she meets a man who dominates her by the mind. In the struggle, it is Gerald the splendid athlete, the jealous, possessive, pathetically physical man who dies. All three of the thoughtful ones are deeply concerned with the demands of their minds. Passion sways them back and forth. One man has dreamed of a love over love, beyond love, so that the mind will remain free. There is no story, and there is no solution, and no end to such dreams. The women live within ideas which mould them, although they are so utterly woman that they do not refrain from giving their bodies. Then one gently endeavors to humanize her over-intellectual man while the other flees from Gerald because he is mindless and just human. But the issues are more obscure than that, and more profound. Without Lawrence's own words one cannot even describe them. We use words in the daily, careless sense. His is a special language, free, informal, extremely personal, to which he gave the power to unite the fantastic and the real. For this reason, and because he returned to the same problem several times, it is best to read

Lawrence as a whole. Lawrence was not the man to be defined by one book, and in one moment. He has a language, a setting, a world entirely his own, and only by a thorough absorption of it can one understand it.

Lawrence is so truthful that he seems at times to lack pity. He seemed to lack pity for the grey, tired city man, the sunless one in "Sun," and for Lady Chatterley's husband, wounded in the war. But he was not concerned with pity—just with truth. Truth itself is pitiless and pitiable. Stories by other men than Lawrence are less finely balanced. The cheated husband is made hateful, so that feeling can go freely to the lovers. Lawrence will not have it so because it is not so. Feeling is all to be divided. Even within one love there is divided feeling; even within one truth there is divided dual truth; life cannot be so easily split, measured, and disposed of. The two men in "England, My England" are both distressingly right, distressingly pitiable, one so responsible, the other so irresponsible and both equally necessary, both harmful, both admirable. Lawrence never weighs. The poetry and the bare truth exist side by side. Pity wavers back and forth, just as ideas do, and convictions. Lawrence knew there was no finality, no solution, no ground one could be certain never to want to move away from. If you are terribly truthful the ground will always move from under you, you will have to shift with shifting truth. You will crave a definite idea (that is our hell), you may worship one, but you will also shift with shifting truth, just as Lawrence did.

Originally published under the pseudonym "Melisendra" in The Canadian Forum *(October 1930), this essay represented Anaïs Nin's first appearance as a writer and served as a springboard for her first book,* D.H. Lawrence: An Unprofessional Study *(Paris, 1932)*

REALISM AND REALITY (1946)

I WANT TO CLARIFY some misunderstandings that have occasionally blocked the response to my work. They arise mostly from the fact that I write as a poet in the framework of prose and appear to claim the rights of a novelist. I deal with characters, it is true, but the best way to approach my way of dealing with them is as one regards modern painting. I intend the greater part of my writing to be received directly through the senses, as one receives painting and music. The moment you begin to look at my writing in terms of modern painting you will be in possession of one key to its meaning and will understand why I have left out so much that you are accustomed to finding in character novels.

There is a purpose and form behind my partial, impressionistic, truncated characters. The whole house, or the whole body, the entire environment, may not be there, but we know from modern painting that a column can signify more than a whole house, and that one eye can convey more than two at times. We know that in Brancusi's sculpture he achieved the closest expression of the flight of a bird by eliminating the wings.

As my books take place in the unconscious, and hardly ever outside of it, they differ from poetry not in tone, language, or rhythm, but merely by the fact that they contain both the symbol and the interpretation of the symbol. The process of distillation, of reduction to the barest essentials, is voluntary because dealing with the chaotic content of the unconscious in the form of the poem is natural, but to poetize and analyze simultaneously is a process which is too elusive and swift to include much upholstery.

If the writing has a dream-like quality it is not because the dramas I present are dreams, but because they are the dramas as the unconscious lives them. I never include the concrete object or fact unless it has a symbolic role to play. As in the dream when a chair appears in my book it is because this chair has something portentous to reveal about the drama that is taking place. Thus alone can I achieve the intensification and vividness of a kind of drama which we know to be highly elusive and fragmentary and which takes place usually only in psychoanalysis.

These dramas of the unconscious to gain a form and validity of their own must temporarily displace the over-obtrusive, dense, deceptive settings of our outer world which usually serve as concealment, so that we may become as familiar with its inner properties and developments as we are with the workings of our conscious, external worlds.

As in Miro's painting, the circus is indicated by a line, a red ball, and space. This conforms to my concept that modern writing must have the swift rhythm of our time, and be as lightly cargoed as the airplane to permit flight and speed. It is my belief that emotionally as well as scientifically, we are going to travel more lightly and that writing will not belong to our time if it does not learn to travel faster than sound!

And how are we going to fly with novels which begin: "She was sitting under a 40 watt Mazda lamp." (The author I will not mention for fear of libel.)

The new investigations of the unconscious have brought people nearer to poetry, for every man knows that he is continuously constructing a dream duplicate of his life in the same symbolic terms used familiarly by the poets and that he too possesses a very subtle and intricate way of dramatizing the concealed meaning of his life.

At night every man dreams in the imagery of the poets, but in the daytime he denies and rejects the world of the artist as if it were not his world, even to the length of classifying such dream activity as symptomatic of neurosis when it is actually a symptom of the creativity latent in every man.

These investigations will also make us more impatient with the opaque quality of our external world which is used in most novels as a defense against a disturbing deeper world, as an obstacle in reaching it, as an obstruction created by fear; and they will produce a greater impatience even with meaningless acts, with all evasions of the essential inner drama practiced by the so-called realistic novel in which we are actually being constantly cheated of reality and experience.

◆

The occasional resistance I have encountered has been due, I believe, to my use of the symbolic, my use of daily objects not as they stand around us as reassuring, consoling solidities, like a cup of coffee, or an alarm clock, but that I come like a magician of doubtful authenticity and transform this cup of coffee and this alarm clock into stage properties for a story which then seems like a dream and not reality.

Yet everyone does this, as we know, every night, whenever he begins to interpret or dramatize the deeper significance of his acts.

Now I place you in a world which is like the world of the dream, sparingly furnished only with the objects which have proved their symbolic value, and not their familiar value as objects which give us our daily gravitational security. It is because I assume that the world of the dream, like the world of my books, is actually the way we re-experience our life, and I expect people to recognize its contours or its lack of contours without fear (the most disturbing element of the dream is that it has no frames, no walls, no doors and no boundaries. . . like my novels). Whatever anxiety my writing may create can only be the anxiety people feel in the presence of an incomplete but highly significant dream.

I cannot claim the privileges granted to the poet (he is allowed his mystery and praised for what he does not reveal) because the poet is content with bringing forth the flow of images but does not set about to interpret them as characters. All mysteries become explicit when they are personified and dramatized, and I tend toward a greater explicitness, but not before the reality of the inner drama is made completely valid in itself.

The conventionalities of the novel can no longer communicate what we know. That is why James Joyce exploded the form of the novel and let his writing erupt in a veritable flow. As Edmund Wilson put it: "Just as Joyce in *Ulysses* laid the *Odyssey* under requisition to help provide a structure for his material—a material which, once it had begun to gush forth from the rock of Joyce's sealed personality at the blow of Aaron's rod of free associations, threatened to rise and submerge the artist like the floods which the sorceress's apprentice let loose by his bedeviled broom."

But there is no need to seek a structure from the old myths. In the human unconscious itself, once unraveled, there is an indigenous structure and pattern. If we are able to detect and seize and use it we have the conflicts and the forms of the novel of the future.

The pattern of the new novel will be one in which everything will be produced only as it is discovered by the emotions: by associations and repetitions, by associative memory as in Proust, by repetitious experiences out of which the meaning finally becomes clear, as it does in life, alone, making it possible to seize the inner pattern and not the false exterior ones. The pattern of the deeper life covered and disguised will be uncovered and demasked by the writer's process of interpretation of the symbolic meaning of people's acts, not a mere reporting of them or of their words. The incoherence of such a way of writing, often practiced by D.H. Lawrence, is only apparent and ceases as soon as the writer strikes the deepest level of all, for the unconscious creates the most consistent patterns and plots of all.

◆

Many novels today include the psychoanalytical experience. That is only a crude makeshift. The novelist knows that psychoanalysis has uncovered layers not uncovered in the narrative novel (particularly in a society where people's acts no longer correspond to their inner impulses; this does not apply, for instance, to the Dostoyevskian novels in which people act by the impulses of their unconscious, as we do not). But so far he has granted this uncovering power only to the professional analyst, not realizing that this power must become an integral part of his novelist's equipment.

Historical knowledge as it was used by a Joyce or a Proust was never introduced into the novel as pure history but as an integrated part of the novelist's total vision. Thus the new perspective of character, as it can be created by the novelist familiar with the unconscious, will be slowly integrated within the novel and will not need to be voiced through a doctor. The novelist has allowed the doctor to do what he felt impotent to do himself, shifting the responsibilities of breaking through false patterns, disguises, thus increasing the reader's feelings that neurosis in a character made it a "case" and not an experience very common in our world today, which it is. The novelist himself has not yet accepted the unconscious activity, the unconscious dramas as an integral part of all characters.

A woman was complaining of her bad health to a friend and this friend said: "With you I'm sure it's not a neurotic complaint."

"Of course not," said the sick woman, "it's not neurotic. It's just human."

If we can accept neurosis as a part of our humanity it will cease to be a "case" in literature and become one of the richest sources of fiction writing.

There is no denying that we are suffering from a collective neurosis and the novel which does not face this is not a novel of our time. Collective neurosis can no longer be dismissed as exceptional, pathological, or decadent. It is a direct result of our social system. As soon as we accept this we are ready to face the causes and to reach into deeper relations to history.

◆

While we refuse to organize the confusions within us we will never have an objective understanding of what is happening outside. We will not be able to relate to it, to choose sides, to evaluate historically, and consequently we will be incapacitated for action. The novelist's preoccupation with inner distortions is not morbid or a love of illness but it comes as a truthful mirror of today's drama. In order to take action full experience is required. All novels which contribute to our emotional atrophy only deepen our blindness. The novels today do not reflect our life but people's fear of life, of experience, of the deeper layers of self-knowledge by which we alone can defeat tragedy.

Reportage, the other extreme from unconscious writing, is not reality either, because facts stated objectively, scientifically, statistically, without the artist's power to communicate their meaning, do not give us an emotional experience. And anything that we do not discover emotionally will not have the power to alter our vision. In reportage we are once more cheated of experience, and realism is substituted for reality.

As soon as I say "experience" there are some who grow afraid again, who think that "experience" means to be first of all everything one writes about. But by experience I do not always mean to act, but to feel. A young writer said to me one day: "I saw a workman who had had his hand torn off by a machine. I didn't feel anything." Such a person is not only schizophrenic, he is no doubt a bad writer. To experience this one does not have to be the workman to whom this happened.

The richest source of creation is feeling, followed by a vision of its meaning. The medium of the writer is not ink and paper but his body: the sensitivity of his eyes, ears, and heart. If these are atrophied let him give up writing.

ON WRITING (1947)

THERE HAS BEEN an attempt to categorize my work as a mere depiction of neurosis, and therefore as dealing with an exceptional rather than a general theme.

But on the contrary, I not only believe that we *are* suffering from a collective neurosis, but that this is precisely one of the most *urgent* themes for the novel today: the struggle between the forces of nature in us and our repressive and consequently destructive treatment of these forces.

This struggle has, for the moment at least, resulted in neurosis, which is simply a form of protest against an unnatural life.

That is why I want to speak about writing not in formal terms, but mainly of *naturalness* in writing, because in the presence of a collective neurosis it is all the more essential for the novelist not to share with the neurotic this paralyzing fear of nature which has been the cause of so much sterility in life and in the writing of today.

I chose to write about neurotic women because women, being closer to nature, have made a more vehement protest against repressions.

Man has faced boldly the forces of nature outside of himself, has investigated them, mastered and harnessed many of them. But this conquest deprived him at the same time of his primitive, intimate contact with nature, resulting in a partial loss of his power and vitality.

Woman has retained her communication with nature (even in its negative form of destruction) and could have remained the symbol of nature for man, because her language and her means of perception are more unconscious and non-rational. But she has failed to fulfill that role, partly because of her tendency to imitate man and adopt his goals, and partly because of man's fear of complete contact with the nature of woman.

Perhaps this fear in man arose from his being not quite so certain that the forces of nature manifested through woman could be as easily mastered or harnessed!

This has led to the absence, or failure, of relationship between men and women so prevalent today, and it is a dramatic proof of the absence of relationship between man and nature.

While we refuse to organize the confusions *within* us we will never have an objective understanding of what is happening *outside*.

We will not be able to relate to it, to choose sides, to evaluate historically, and consequently we will be incapacitated for *action*.

Today a novelist's preoccupation with inner psychological distortions does not stem from a morbid love of illness but from a knowledge that this is the *theme* of our new reality.

◆

Like the modern physicist the novelist of today should face the fact that this new psychological reality can be explored and dealt with only under conditions of tremendously high atmospheric pressures, temperatures and speed, as well as in terms of new time-space dimensions for which the old containers represented by the traditional forms and conventions of the novel are completely inadequate and inappropriate.

That is why James Joyce shattered the old form of the novel and let his writing erupt in a veritable flow of associations.

Most novels today are inadequate because they reflect *not our experience*, but people's fear of experience. They portray all the *evasions*.

I believe that the experience of war might have been less disastrous to the mental and emotional life of young Americans if they had been prepared by an honest literature for all the deep primitive experience with birth, sex, and death.

In order to take action full maturity in experience is required. Novels which contribute to our emotional atrophy only deepen our blindness.

And nothing that we do not discover *emotionally* will have the power to alter our vision.

The constant evasion of emotional experience has created an immaturity which turns all experience into traumatic shocks from which the human being derives no strength or development, but neurosis.

Frederick Hoffman, writing about D.H. Lawrence, says: "Lawrence sensed a definite danger that the novel might deaden the senses and simply present dead matter persisting in a dead world. But if it is handled as a live portrait it is at once the artist's most fluid medium and his best opportunity to convey to the world the *meaning* of the world, `the changing rainbow of our living relationships` How can creative art accomplish this? Life is so fluid that one can only hope to capture the living moment, to capture it alive and fresh—not the ordinary moment of an ordinary day but the critical moment of human relationships. How to capture this

oscillation within the prison of cold print, without destroy-
ing that movement?"

It was while writing a diary that I discovered how to capture the living moments. Keeping a diary all my life helped
me to discover some basic elements essential to the vitality
of writing.

When I speak of the relationship between my diary and
writing I do not intend to generalize as to the value of keeping a diary, or to advise anyone to do so, but merely to extract from this habit certain discoveries which can be easily
transposed to other kinds of writing.

Of these, the most important is naturalness and spontaneity. These elements sprung, I observed, from my freedom
of selection: in the diary I only wrote of what interested me
genuinely, what I felt most *strongly* at the moment, and I
found that this fervor, this enthusiasm produced a vividness which often withered in the formal work. Improvisa-
tion, free association, obedience to mood, impulse, brought
forth countless images, portraits, descriptions, impressionistic sketches, symphonic experiments, into which I could
dip at any time for material.

The diary, dealing always with the immediate present,
the warm, the near, being written at white heat, developed a
love of the living moment, the immediate emotional reaction to experience, which revealed the power of recreation

to lie in the sensibilities rather than in memory or critical intellectual perception.

The diary, creating a vast tapestry, a web, exposing constantly the relation between the past and present, weaving meticulously the invisible interaction, noting the repetitions of themes, developed the sense of the totality of personality. This tale without beginning or end, which encloses all things, and relates all things, was a strong antidote to the unrelatedness, incoherence, and disintegration of modern man. I could follow the inevitable pattern and obtain a large, panoramic view of character.

This personal relationship to all things, which is condemned as subjective, limiting, I found to be the core of individuality, personality, and originality. The idea that subjectivity is an impasse is as false as the idea that objectivity leads to a larger form of life.

A deep personal relationship reaches far beyond the personal into the general. Again it is a matter of depths.

The diary also taught me that it is in the moments of emotional crisis that human beings reveal themselves most accurately. I learned to choose the heightened moments because they are the moments of revelation. It is the moment when the real self rises to the surface, shatters its false roles, erupts and assumes reality and identity. The fiery moments of passionate experience are the moments of wholeness and totality of the personality.

By this emphasis on the fiery moments, the explosions, I reached the reality of feeling and the senses.

◆

The split from reality, fragmentation, the dismemberment of modern man has been the theme of modern literature, beginning with Marcel Proust's microscopic analysis, through the dissolutions of Joyce's undifferentiated flow of association, but neither of these processes needed to prove fatal. The discovery of the collective richness flowing underground below our consciousness need not have led to a loss of the total self. But what remains to be done is a new synthesis to include the new dimensions discovered.

The new dimension in character and reality requires a fusion of two extremes which have been handled separately, on the one side by the poets, and on the other by the so-called realists.

I am not saying that I have done it.

I actually think it will be accomplished by the younger, unpublished writers I have been reading.

Diary writing also taught me that to achieve perfection in writing, while retaining naturalness, it was important to write a great deal, to write fluently, as the pianist practices the piano, rather than to correct constantly one page until it withers. To write continuously, to try over and over again to capture a certain mood, a certain experience. Intensive correcting may lead to monotony, to working on dead matter, whereas continuing to write, and to write until perfection is achieved through repetition, is a way to elude this monotony, to avoid performing an autopsy. Sheer playing of scales, practice, repetition—then by the time one is ready to write a story or a novel a great deal of natural distillation and sorting has been accomplished.

◆

There is another great danger for the writer, perhaps the greatest one of all: his consciousness of the multiple taboos society has imposed on literature, and his inner censor. In the diary I found a devious (a woman's) way to evade this outer and inner censor. It is surprising how well one writes if one thinks no one will read you.

This honesty, this absence of posturing, is a most fecund source of material. The writer's task is to overthrow the taboos rather than accept them.

With all my insistence on the overthrow of outworn taboos, I nevertheless respected the power of art.

Naked truth is unbearable to most, and art is our most effective means of overcoming human resistance to truth. The writer has the same role as the surgeon, and his handling of anaesthesia is as important as his skill with the knife.

Human beings, in their resistance to truth, erect fortresses and some of these fortresses can only be demolished by the dynamic power of the symbol, which reaches the emotions directly.

D.H. Lawrence says: "Symbols don't *mean* something, they *are* units of human experience. A complex of emotional experience *is* a symbol. And the power of the symbol is to arouse the deep, emotional, dynamic, primitive self."

The fact that man persists in dreaming in terms of symbols shows how he clings to this primitive emotional perception.

◆

It is even more interesting to talk about what has not yet been done.

For instance, I believe a rich fund of symbolism lies in science. The old romantic symbols no longer correspond to our reality.

Modern science is giving birth to symbols which parallel the new psychological realities, and could make their tenuous patterns more concrete.

I can't do it because I know too little about science!

My studies led me rather toward language and art.

Having come to America as a foreigner, and not knowing English, I caught a new perspective of the language.

But whatever marvelous world I unearthed from the dictionary with the enthusiasm of an explorer was always condemned to disuse by my English teacher as obsolete or affected. When I asked: Who proclaimed them so?, she could not answer me. It was this prim evasiveness which led me to suspect that much of this mysterious censorship of expansiveness in language had been caused by Puritanism: a puritanical disapprobation of richness, a puritanical fear of color, a puritanical shame of the senses and suspicion of charm.

Coming from Spain it struck me that we had forgotten in America how masterfully the ancients used charms to encourage salvation.

Whoever has smelled incense in a church will admit that religion made a wise use of *olfactory enchantments*.

Are we going to discard all these forms of communication and persuasion because they were sometimes mishandled?

Whoever has read the *Arabian Nights* knows how much art has to do here with enlivening the energies! Art is our relation to the senses.

The great potency of ancient tales, legends, ballads, lay in their power to prepare the senses for the magic effect of the tale.

This sounds as if I were recommending hypnotism. If the sound of Joyce's voice reading the chanting quality of his rhythms is hypnotic then I say: better be hypnotized than die in the deserts of bare and barren writing.

The inciting to naturalness immediately brings up the problem of form.

By following rigorously and exclusively the patterns made by the emotions I found that in the human unconscious itself there is an indigenous structure, and if we are able to detect and grasp it we have the plot, the form, and style of the novel of the future.

In this apparently chaotic world of the unconscious there is an inevitability as logical, as coherent, as final as any to be found in classical drama.

In this new dimension of character the form is created by the meaning, it is born of the theme. It is created very much as the earth itself is created, by a series of inner convulsions and eruptions, dictated by inner geological tensions. It is an organic development.

For instance, when I began the portrait of Stella I had no premeditated plan, but the character of Stella being a summation of the feminine spirit—labyrinthean, elusive, and mobile, this gave to the writing itself its contours, its rhythms. The writing was determined by the form of her nature, it reflected the tonalities of her voice. I instinctively chose lightweight words to match the volatility of her gestures, words of the same substance as her moods and mannerisms.

I would like to give now an example of how creative the unconscious can be if one allows it to work spontaneously.

◆

In *Ladders to Fire* I had written the section called "This Hunger" up to the description of an impasse in the relationship between Jay and Lillian: because she has to mother the child in him, she cannot have a real child. She surrenders the human child and accepts her role.

And there I stopped for a few days.

One morning I awakened to remember a concert I had heard in Paris years ago. The memory came up with great vividness and persistence. I was a little annoyed for it had no apparent connection with what I was writing and I looked on it as an irrelevant interruption.

But it confronted me with the clarity and precision of a painting and to rid myself of its hauntingness I decided to write it down. The concert itself was not what had made a lasting impression on me but the strange sight I had caught as I looked out through a big bay window into a garden: three large mirrors had been placed in the center of the garden. The incongruity of mirrors in a garden was striking, but such a scene only stirs a deep response when it touches off some primitive recognition of a symbolic drama.

As I wrote on, about the woman pianist, about the real garden, and its reflection in the mirror I still wondered why the impression had been deep enough to last for years, and why it should have come to the surface of my memory at this particular moment. It was only when I was finished writing that I realized I had continued the story of "This Hunger" and completed it by giving the key to the book: the woman pianist playing with such intensity was trying to divert a natural instinct (the need of a human child) into music.

But the transmutation was not being made.

The real garden represented nature, relaxed, fulfilled. The mirrors—neurosis, reflection, artifice.

The mirrors in the garden were the perfect symbol of unreality and refraction, a miniature reproduction of the drama I had been portraying of a conflict between nature and neurosis.

THE WRITER
AND THE SYMBOLS

I AM OFTEN ASKED: how is a story born?

The creation of a story is a *quest for meaning*. The objects, the incidents, the characters are always there, as they are for the painter, but the key which catalyzes is the relation between the exterior and interior drama. The significance *is* the drama. The meaning is what illumines the facts, coordinates them, incarnates them. For example: once I found myself in the ancient city of Antigua. Everything around me was romantic, dramatic, picturesque. All the elements to compose a story. A volcano, Mayan ruins, Mayan costumes, mysteriously silent people. Yet none of these, compiled, tabulated, would create a story. They would only produce a travelogue. For three days I wandered through the city knowing I possessed no key to it, no story. Then I heard about a woman who had wanted to take a sun bath on one of the terraces and had been attacked by a vulture. Following this I observed the vultures, and then the strange fact that there were no birds singing, that the extraordinary muteness of the air was what gave Antigua its static quality. The keynote of Antigua was death. Once I knew death was the theme of the city of Antigua I was able to gather together all the elements, images, moods of the city, and when I became aware completely of the atmosphere of the city I also saw for the first time the similar characteristic between the people who chose to live there, the group of Americans who lived a static, arrested form of life there. Without this illumination from within, you obtain nothing but a still life. With this key one can go as deeply and as far as one wishes by pushing the association of ideas further: why was the symbol of vultures, of silence, so apt to describe Antigua? Did the external semblance of death, the ruins, correspond to an internal one? The silence of the Mayan Indians was like death, as if the volcanic eruption which had destroyed their city long ago had truly buried the living too. The people who were attracted to live there seemed also to have reached an impasse in their lives. The theme of death could be developed to infinity, reaching back and forth into the past and into the present, into the personal and the historical.

◆

The craft of writing can include all the others. A writer can possess the eye of a painter as Proust did, the ear of a musi-
n as Joyce did, the rhythm of a dancer as Isabel Bolton's

prose has in *Do I Wake or Sleep*. He can possess the antennae of a clairvoyant, as Isak Dinesen did in her book on Africa; the prophetic qualities of a fortune teller as Huxley did in *Brave New World*. He can have the sense of form of a sculptor, the knowledge of textures of a dress designer, an eye for scenic arrangements of the stage director. He has to be an architect to house his characters, an entomologist, a botanist. He needs all the arts and sciences to reveal all the aspects of man. He must be a subtle detective of man's hidden character since we now know that all men are their own impersonators, and that the so-called realists who believed they were copying natural man were only copying man's impersonations, the protective persons by which he carefully concealed his deepest self.

The accelerated *rhythm* of our modern life could not be without its counterpart in literature. This demands a greater condensation. The true meaning, the true purpose of abstraction is not a dehydration of experience, but an extracting and distilling of its essence to achieve greater intensity.

There are also perceptions which can only be communicated by *rhythm*, the cadences of a mood, the cadences of speech, the life pulse as in jazz music. Poetic writing is not alone used for decorative purposes. By rhythm, repetitions, symphonic composition, the actual pulse of living is sensed as by contagion and the emotion penetrates the bloodstream.

When I say I have composed musically, or as a painter, I might also add that I have composed by following and obeying the dictates of life rhythms and moods, by an exaggeration of words, by attrition, by accumulation, by organic cellular growth of both ideas and feelings, obeying above all the laws of spontaneity and enthusiasm.

I never, for example, write about something which bores me, in which I am not interested, because the emotion with which one writes is by contagion felt by the one who reads. The bored, indifferent writer conveys his boredom and indifference even when he is not aware of it.

Every writer experiences moments of paralysis, of stagnation, when the work seems completely blocked. I have found these obstacles to be more often psychological than technical. I have analyzed my own blockages and asked myself: what am I afraid of? Of transgressing taboos which will bring retaliation and criticism? Do I fear ridicule? Do I feel the theme too intricate, too difficult for me? Is it a childhood fear of the consequences of being truthful? Of hurting others? Of revealing secrets which do not belong to us? There are so many fears. We fear exposure of self even when we are not writing about ourselves. Technical difficulties are often related to psychological difficulties: timidity, indecision, tension, all affect writing. The writer's consciousness of the multiple taboos society has imposed on literature is one obstacle, the other is his own inner censor. The solution to these obstacles lies in artistry and taste. There is always a way of saying the truth in a palatable way, of revealing the most profound layers of experience, and symbolism is one of our defences against the organized persecution of truth. *Art is our most effective way of overcoming human resistance to truth.*

◆

Modern art is a return to the *symbol*, and the symbol is an acknowledgment of the emotional and spiritual content of every act and of every object around us. It is the decoding of this content which should become for us a marvellous stimulant to our intelligence and our sense of adventure and exploration. Our Western life has become mechanical, functional, and devoid of meaning. There is no going back but there *is* the possibility of investing the present with meaning by excavating for depths which get submerged by surface activity, and by maintaining a balance between the emotional and the spiritual so that they can nourish each other. Man's unconscious has remained rich in images and feelings despite all external pressure in the opposite direction. He has not become a robot, but he is in danger of becoming inarticulate if he accepts an impoverishment of language, an oversimplification of relationships to others.

If such symbolic writing appears at first esoteric it is only because if reflects a spiritual underground life of which most people are unaware, and it is unfortunate that they usually only become aware of its existence when, by excessive denial and repression, it grows distorted into neurosis and begins to fester like an abscess of the soul.

The new investigations of the unconscious will bring people nearer to poetry, for every man knows now that he is continually constructing a dream duplicate of his life in exactly the same symbolic imagery familiarly used by the poets, and that he too possesses a very subtle way of dramatizing the concealed, the mysterious meaning of his life and character.

◆

Today a novelist's preoccupation with inner psychological disturbances does not stem from any interest in illness but from the knowledge that we are suffering from a collective neurosis revealed and manifested in war.

Modern man stands in danger of losing his identity, as Kafka so well dramatized in his novels, and he seeks to recapture this lost core of himself through a return to the deeper layers of his personality not yet destroyed by modern life.

There is a new dimension in character and in reality.

Symbolism has another power: naked truth is unbearable to most and art is our most effective way of overcoming human resistance to truth. Human beings barricade themselves against the truth, erect fortresses, and some of these fortresses can only be demolished by the dynamic power of the symbol which penetrates the emotions directly.

Facts stated objectively, without the artist's power to illumine their meaning, do not give us an emotional experience, and nothing that we do not discover by way of feeling has the power to alter our lives. It is, for example, a well known fact that no neurosis was ever helped by the intellectual study of all the books written on psychology. The only effective cure is achieved by an emotional, personal experience with analysis and the analyst.

Contemporary writing may appear mystifying or obscure. Henry James's *Turn of the Screw*, Djuna Barnes's *Nightwood*, are challenges to man's imagination and power of interpretation. Such a challenge should be sought, for it saves the mind from atrophy, from mediocrity. Man's feeling of the loss of centrality and core is due to his abdication of the personal integrity which makes him a living, dynamic, clearsighted part of a whole.

This quest of the self through the intricate maze of modern confusion is the central theme of my work. But you cannot reach unity and integration without patiently experiencing first of all all the turns of the labyrinth of falsities and delusions in which man has lost himself. And you can transcend the personal not by avoiding it, but by confronting it and coming to terms with it.

Symbolism and fantasy has also appeared to many as a form of escape from reality, and was often attacked as a palliative or a drug. But the analyst knows that it is only in this territory that the real or secret man can be captured. We often refer to the magic power of legends, myths, fairy tales, but we never ask ourselves why they had such an enduring power, which no development in science was ever able to dissolve. But it was science itself, Freudism, which proved that they contained the greatest component of man's true existence and that only because they corresponded to his deepest truth did they endure. Even in the light of the coldest analysis, the dream of man dramatizes wishes deeply necessary to him, which he disguised later, or betrayed, but could not entirely destroy.

That is why all my books end with a return to the dream, not as an escape, but as a key to the character. I describe many times, in various ways, the loss of the true self in relationships, and the return to the source where the genuine self lies imbedded.

Another disturbing aspect of *symbolic* writing: it has a meaning we cannot always seize with our intelligence, dissect or even articulate. It has a permeating, a contagious, a flooding quality as music has, if only we allowed it to ferment in us without fear. We have no confidence in the magic power of truth as the primitive had confidence in his magicians.

The most constructive quality of writing which seeks to reveal the depths of character is that once we have learned what patterns in the character have created the dramatic experience, we learn simultaneously that one is free to create a character as often as one has the courage to cast off distortions and falsities. Even in a world of chaos there is a possibility of personal order, which will in turn affect the larger one. Even in a world of conflict and war, there is the possibility of harmony in personal relationships, which will in turn infect the relationship between nations.

When I say that to reach wholeness it is first of all necessary to clarify personal distortions, I do not mean that we need to remain focused on the personal, but that while we refuse to recognize the confusions within us we will never have an objective understanding of what is happening outside. We will not be able to relate to it, to choose sides, to evaluate. Only when the inner lens of our vision is clear can we act toward a larger order and creation. That is why I believe subjective writing is valuable and necessary.

◆

The irrational, the unconscious we know now is the most powerful element in our character, but like all the elements of nature it can be charted, explored, understood and con-quered. As an example of the perfectly lucid treatment of the irrational in fiction there is *Asylum Piece* by Anna Kavan, a little-known writer who has written about irrational char-acters in the most lucid, clairvoyant, compassionate way, so that their motivations appear as clearly to our minds, and as deserving of sympathy, as the most ordinary familiar char-acter around us. To say that such explorations are danger-ous or abnormal is like saying we will not try to climb Annapurna because we might freeze our fingers, or we will not adventure into the Brazilian jungle because of malaria. All adventure, all exploration has its risks but they are no greater than the risk of living a constricted life which stifles our imagination, no more dangerous than accepting a stan-dardized life which does not fit our temperament. In fact, we also know that repression can cause much greater dam-age than that suffered in adventure: it can cause delinquency, crime, neurosis and psychosis. We can adventure into any realm whatever with sufficient courage and insight. And today the adventurers of the spirit should cease to fear the irrational and realize it is the source of great richness. Such knowledge defeats the static concept of fatality. *Our fate is what we call our character.* The more we know about this char-acter the more able we are to direct our destiny and reach our fullest development. But where are the daring explorers of our inner world? We have deep sea divers, we have men willing to descend into caves to chart the geological stratas of the earth, we have scientists eager to reach other planets, but few aside from doctors and a few novelists have been willing to plunge into the unexplored territory of our irrational life. The artist has created from this source and thereby earned quite a little mistrust from the average man. And because the irrational and the unconscious were the springs of art, the artist himself indulged in an unconventional behavior which may have seemed incomprehensible to some, but which in many cases issued from a deeper integrity and sincerity about his wishes and true nature. This is why I chose to write about artists. I was interested in those who had chosen to live by their impulses rather than those who had to fit themselves into accepted social patterns.

◆

Some writers have brought the *irrational* streams into visibility, but like reporters unable to extract either philosophical or psychological deductions from their findings, they emptied their vast nets filled with chaos and threw debris and absurd juxtapositions at our feet. This was what they had found at the bottom of their unconscious. But few gave this a form, a meaning, sifting it and rearranging it with intelligence. They left it all for us to interpret. I am thinking now of many of the surrealist writers. The surrealists brought up much material of this kind. The next step for us was to analyze this material as we presented it.

But we cannot expect all of it to be clear at once, anymore than the mysteries of nature. These are the mysteries of our nature, but recently opened by Freud.

This inner world is almost in opposition to our surface world. It is first of all ruled by flow (as life itself), it has a different design and organization. Again it can be compared with jazz. It is unwritten music in the sense that it is constantly being improvised: it is ruled by free association of ideas and images. Most of it is not clear to the intelligence, but extremely perceptible and audible to the emotions. This is the sign of its authenticity: if it comes from the hidden sources, it touches our feelings. Only by the seismograph of the emotions could one distinguish the authentic unconscious from the artificial one. In 1949 a book was published by New Directions and presented as the first surrealist work in America: John Hawkes's *The Cannibal*, which proves that writers at times can be counterfeiters, quite capable of counterfeiting an unconscious (a soul, a creative or poetic power). The artist as well as any man is capable of stealing what he cannot create. But if we have many counterfeiters there are few explorers, few who will risk frozen feet at the hands of reviewers, fewer still willing to explore the hidden jungles of what Martha Graham called the "dark realms of the heart."

The heroes of the unconscious are few, but they have been adequately reviled: Freud, Proust and Joyce, Kafka, Djuna Barnes. There is no adventure without danger.

◆

Man was examined, displayed and fragmented—but only as other elements were under scientific experiments, only in order to examine these separate fragments: with the Proustian microscope, with the Joycean word mirrors, with new instruments of all kinds we never possessed before—relativity of truth and depth analysis. Man was never whole in the old sense of the word, as we thought any rational being was. But he is whole in a different way than we knew: we have only to make new correlations, a new reassembling to reach a much deeper truth about the nature of man. We seem to have backtracked lately and it was because the discoveries of Freud were a shock to our conventional souls and we preferred to hide ourselves in the myth of a collective community which could function with human beings who had abdicated their individual existence. We know now that this is not so.

We use outworn words and outworn values and discarded definitions to hamper the work of the artist such as no scientist would use when at work upon a new discovery. Every discovery has its new language. We continue to apply to man's character definitions totally trite and empty of meaning. There is today a different concept of wholeness, a different way of integrating and of maturing. Our anxiety will cease with the discovery of our power to guide ourselves from within our own center and true core of being. The effect of this upon the community will then make the community stronger and more intelligent.

First published in ANAÏS: An International Journal, *Volume 4, 1986. An earlier, somewhat different version appeared in* Two Cities *(Paris, April 15, 1959)*

MURDER ON THE PLACE DU TERTRE

M Y COUSIN EDUARDO tells me: "In Nice, I arrived by the same boat which takes the prisoners to Devil's Island. And I was thinking of it for days, how strange it would be if I should sail back with them as a murderer. These two girls and I, after an all night round, returned by taxi. One of the girls kept after me to be careful, not to let myself get cheated. When we arrived the sum the driver asked seemed too high. By that time I was very angry. I argued with him. We came to an agreement. I said I thought he was right after all. And then suddenly I leaped forward and tried to strangle him. What a feeling: his neck in my hands—so soft. I came to my senses. He made as if to get his revolver. I was frightened. It ended there. Those two murders, Noziere and the movie man (reported in the press), they relieved thousands of people who wanted to commit murder. The reprobate is only the Christ who takes on himself the sins of the world. If I commit murder I only put into action the desire of a thousand people."

Anaïs: "You have all the possibilities for becoming a fine reprobate! You are full of malice and deviltry. Let yourself go. If you had let yourself go, you would not have wanted to commit murder."

Eduardo: "But my father—and the money. I will be left to starve."

Anaïs: "You will never starve. You can always come here for rice. The money is only an excuse. It isn't that which stands in the way of your liberation. It's your own fear."

Eduardo: "I have only been half a reprobate until now. I must make a choice. I must go to one excess or the other. Either become a monk or a devil. And I am afraid of letting go because it will mean retrogression—homosexuality, infantilism."

Anaïs: "There are forms of destructiveness which are not regressions."

Eduardo asked Hugh's sanction as of a father. And his green eyes were very long. All the malice in Eduardo has crystallized before me these last months. It was so subtle and secretive I had not realized it—how he likes to see things tangled and terrible; how he pricks all faith with irony; how he brings into relief the defects of people; how he pounces on their vulnerable spot with cold curiosity; how he wishes to see hatred and misery and failure around him; how he dissects until all things shrivel up; his monstrous jealousy and envy. But we knew he would not act. He would neither commit murder, nor write a book. He would sit all life long talking, until he becomes insane.

◆

He was drunk, in a high mood. At midnight, he urged us to go to Paris. The *"Lapin Agile,"* on the precipitous Montmartre hill, like heather on a rock side. A room built of granified smoke and human breath. A wooden Christ, pock-marked by vultures. Gusts of weary, petrified songs—so dusty with use, and worn with overuse. Faces like empty glasses.

The crowds have gone and we have come when the evening is closing tight, like a fan. We are shipwrecked on the Place du Tertre, with those houses which are always about to crumble, or to slide away like a cardboard setting.

Two waiters and two girls are passing, the waiters with their arms around the women. Three policemen are watching. We hear a loud ringing, so loud and insistent the policemen begin to run. What is it, fire, a murder? I say to Eduardo: "Someone has committed your murder." The two waiters and the women run after the policemen. The loud ringing continues. It comes from a telephone on the sidewalk. The policeman answers: *"Mais non, mais non, soyez tranquille. Tout est bien calme, absolumment calme!"*

We three laugh, laugh in the calm night, in the calm Place du Tertre.

We pass by a cabaret which is also vomiting its adepts. It is called "Ton-Ton"—and many gays come out, swinging their hips, and tidying their curled hair. A woman shouts: "*Au revoir mon choux!*" I am sitting in the back of the car and I wail: "Oh, I want a *choux* too. Give me a *choux—a choux à la crème*, with curly hair and a *phoque* around his neck." I pronounce *phoque*: "fuck."

Eduardo and Hugh are full of cognac, and they are sad. My belly is empty, but I am full of gaiety, singing my song about the *choux* with a *phoque* around his neck. Hugh sees my image in the mirror of the car and thinks: She looks like that, and she laughs like that when she is out with Henry.

Eduardo tries Hugh's neck and mine, to see if they are soft. He is waiting for the drama which only comes from one's own entrails. He is looking to see if it comes through the open doors.

Fragment from the diary, October 16, 1933. First published in
ANAÏS: An International Journal, *Volume 11, 1993*

"THE WHITE BLACKBIRD"

CONFINED BY THE STRAITJACKET, he smiled with a puzzled expression and looked down at his crossed arms and paralyzed legs. He was still completely out of breath from the struggle to escape from the white-coated men who held him. He himself was wearing the white coat and white hat of a chef.

Looking at him ironically, the doctor said, "Why are you so angry? Why are you struggling so hard? What are you afraid of?"

The cook hesitated.

"Well! It's because you had everything ready to deprive me of my strength. The white blackbird is born only once every hundred years and is on the side of Good. The man in the white tie who warned me of the risk I was running belonged to the Order of the White Blackbirds, those who are born every hundred years and are on the side of Good. The white blackbird entered into me and that is why the haddocks are pursuing me. They are on the side of Evil and they have it in for me. There are six of them and sometimes they drive by in a carriage—that is, they used to drive by in a carriage, as in the etching I saw. Of course, today they drive a car and they chase me to deprive me of my strength. The president died today or else I wouldn't be here."

"But the president is not dead."

"Perhaps not, but then it was someone else who looks just like him. There is always someone who looks just like us, who thinks the same as we do, like the girl who thinks like me, the fiancee that I lost."

"Does your fiancee know you are here?"

"Not yet, but she certainly will know, since she thinks like me and the same things happen to her. That's why I am being pursued by the men and the castrated priest who sometimes appears in the form of a woman."

"Where did you see the priest?"

"Why, in the mirror! He pretends to be a woman, but he is a priest they castrated, just as you wanted to castrate me a while ago because I wanted the girl who thinks like me. Because there are more haddocks than white blackbirds and they are black and jealous. And those who are on the side of Good are always persecuted by six men dressed in gray who drive by in a carriage—or, if you prefer, in an automobile, since that is the custom nowadays."

"How do you recognize the white blackbird?"

"By its thoughts."

"You have tried to kill yourself, haven't you?"

"Yes, because no body loves me. I was sent down to live the life of the poet Alfred de Musset, who suffered a great deal, as you know, because nobody loved him. I was sent to live Musset's life and to explain what he prophesied before he hanged himself."

"Ah, Musset hanged himself?"

"Of course, but no one knows it and I have been sent to defend his honor."

"How are you going to defend his honor?"

"By explaining the prophecy that he uttered in a café just before closing time, when he stood in front of the mirror waving a towel as the Angelus rang."

"Why the Angelus?"

"Because I was born while the Angelus was ringing."

He smiled delicately. "I know very well you don't believe what I am telling you. You think I read all this in a mystery story. It's true, I've read a thousand novels because I bore the bruises of love. That girl who was my exact counterpart didn't love me, and I threw myself into the Nile, in Egypt. She always wanted to know the source of my strength, which came from the white blackbird who entered into me and which you want to take away. When one is white, one always has enemies, and I have many. There are many more haddocks than white blackbirds."

The doctor turned to me. "You see, he's incoherent. It doesn't make sense, it isn't logical. It's a clearly defined case of schizophrenia, with disassociation of the ideas. He has a persecution complex."

The cook laughed softly.

"That's funny, isn't it! But that's how it is. And I am not telling you a mystery story."

The two aides, who watched over him so that he wouldn't become dangerous, knew that he couldn't take a single step without falling down. When the doctor told him that he might go, they let him stand up and take two steps toward the door, while the doctor looked on, smiling. They let him take two steps and fall down. The doctor was allowed to continue smiling, proud of his own logic; the madman was allowed to fall, and God allowed him to say all those things about the white blackbird. It was a little bit like the road to Calvary.

Translated from the French by Jean L. Sherman. "Le Merle Blanc"
first appeared in The Booster *(Paris, September 1937)*

LOU ANDREAS-SALOME—
THE FIRST MODERN WOMAN

T HE LACK OF a complete knowledge of Lou Andreas-Salome's life forces our imagination to interpret her in the light of a woman's struggle for independence. We can accept the mysteries, ambivalences, and contradictions because they are analogous to the state of our knowledge of woman today. There is much to be filled in about the inner motives and reactions, the subconscious drives of women. History and biography have to be rewritten. We do not possess yet a feminine point of view in evaluating women because of so many years of taboos on revelations. Women were usually punished by society and by the critics for such revelations as they did attempt. The double standard in biographies of women was absolute.

Lou Andreas-Salome symbolizes the struggle to transcend conventions and traditions in ideas and in living. How can an intelligent, creative, original woman relate to men of genius without being submerged by them? The conflict of the woman's wish to merge with the loved one but to maintain a separate identity is the struggle of modern woman. Lou lived out all the phases and evolution of love, from giving to withholding, from expansion to contraction. She married and led a non-married life, she loved both older and younger men. She was attracted to talent but did not want to serve merely as a disciple or a muse. Nietzsche admitted writing *Zarathustra* under her inspiration; he said that she understood his work as no one else did.

For many years she suffered the fate of brilliant women associated with brilliant men: she was known only as the friend of Nietzsche, Rilke, Freud, even though the publication of her correspondence with Freud showed with what equality he treated her and how he sought her opinion with respect. She made the first feminist study of Ibsen's women and a study of Nietzsche's work. But most of her books are not in print, and few, if any, available in English.

If she inspired Rilke, she also rebelled against his dependency and his depressions. Her love of life was weighed down, and finally, after six years, she broke with him because as she said: "I cannot be faithful to others, only to myself." She had her own work to do, and her faithfulness was to her expansive nature, her passion for life and her work. She awakened others' talents, but maintained a space for her own. She behaved as did all the strong personalities of her time whose romantic attachments we all admired when they were men. She had a talent for friendship and love but she was not consumed by the passions of the romantics which made them prefer death to the loss of love. Yet she inspired romantic passions. She was in attitude, thought, and work, way ahead of her time.

It was natural that Lou should fascinate me, haunt me. But I wondered what Lou would mean to a young woman, a creative and modern young woman. That is when I decided to discuss Lou with Barbara Kraft who writes in a study of Lou: "During the span of Salome's life (1861-1937) she witnessed the close of the romantic tradition and became a part of the evolution of modern thought which came to fruition in the twentieth century. Salome was the first 'modern woman.' The nature of her talks with Nietzsche and Rilke anticipated the philosophical position of existentialism. And through her work with Freud she figured prominently in the early development and practice of psychoanalytical theory. I began to see her as a heroine—as a person worthy of hero worship in its most positive aspects. Women today suffer tremendously from a lack of identification with a heroic feminine figure."

Barbara felt that the feminine heroic figures hardly existed because their biographies were usually written by men.

We discussed why Lou Andreas-Salome moved from one relationship to another. We would see that as a very young woman she feared the domination of Nietzsche who was seeking a disciple, one who would perpetuate his work. After woman she feared the domination of Nietzsche who was seeking a disciple, one who would perpetuate his work. After reading her letters to Rilke, we could understand why after six years she felt she had fulfilled her relationship to Rilke and had to move on. She showed remarkable persistence in maintaining her identity. Gently and wisely she expressed feminine insights in her discussions with Freud and he came to respect her judgment. She preserved her autonomy while surrounded by powerful, even overpowering men. Because she was a beautiful woman their interest often shifted from admiration to passion; when she did not respond she was termed frigid. Her freedom consisted in acting out her deep unconscious needs. She saw independence as the only way to achieve movement. And for her movement was constant growth and evolution. She took her pattern of life from men but she was not a masculine woman. She demanded the freedom to change, to evolve, to grow. She asserted her integrity against the sentimentality and hypocritical definitions of loyalties and duties. She is unique in the history of her time. She was not a feminist at all, but struggling against the feminine side of herself in order to maintain her integrity as an individual.

From the preface to the paperback edition of My Sister, My Spouse. *A Biography of Lou Andreas-Salome, by H.F. Peters (New York: W.W. Norton, 1974)*

THE RELEVANCE
OF DR. OTTO RANK

From the Preface to "La Volonté du Bonheur"

T O F U L L Y R E C O G N I Z E the relevance and contemporary quality of Dr. Otto Rank's work it is important to
know the vital impulses which directed his thoughts toward
the future.

First of all it was the work of a rebel, a man who stood in
a symbolic father-son relation to Freud, and who dared to
diverge from his theories. Such a challenge to an already
established and crystallized dogma is usually punished by
repression, which is exactly what happened to Dr. Otto Rank.
The disciples of Freud pursued a relentless excommunica-
tion which is only dying today with the men who practiced
it. Otto Rank was erased from the history of psychoanalysis
and from public evaluations of psychoanalytical movements.
He himself prophesized that it would take fifty years for a
true understanding of his work. He miscalculated . . .

The second vital factor was that Otto Rank was a poet, a
novelist, a playwright. When he examined the creative per-

sonality it was not only as a psychologist, but as a literary man, as is evident in the book *Art and Artist*. In this study of creativity we can see how he adapted the creative principles beyond the arts to the art of living. It is characteristic of Otto Rank that in his own introduction to *La Volonté du Bonheur* he writes: "This study deals with life and not just with knowledge." (*"Cette etude il faut la vivre et non pas la connaitre."*)*

Volonté du Bonheur concentrates on "the creation of the individual," who "in the ideal case, (becomes) creator himself, (of) his own personality."

It is necessary to stress this because these elucidations were at first believed to concern only the neurotic, but as we have witnessed the failure of collective ideals and mass movements (made up of individually blind numbers, they could only achieve disaster and become the robots of the power principles) it became vitally necessary to recognize the wisdom of individual insight and will power to resist destructive influences.

"It is the strength of this primitive force inside the individual which we will call will." (*C'est la vigeur de cette force primitive representée dans l'individu que nous appellons volonté.*)

The theme of this book is more important today than ever. Science has expanded our universe and thrown us into con-

*Rank's "Avertissement" appeared in the first French edition of *Wahrheit und Wirklichkeit* (1929), translated from the German by Yves Le Lay, published in 1934 by Editions Stock. It was omitted from the English versions (*Truth and Reality*, first published in 1936 in Jessie Taft's translation, now available as a W.W. Norton paperback), but retained in the 1975 reprint by Editions Stock, which also contained a French version of this "Preface."—Ed.

cepts of space beyond our human understanding. Expanding the universe without expanding our inner perceptions becomes for modern man the dangerous experience of void, of emptiness. He is detached from the last remnants of his self and thrown into orbit without hope of returning to his human center. Science and technology, on the other hand, have made man passive. They have insidiously corroded his creative powers, his power to create works and to create himself. Modern man, oppressed by vast mass movements, mass education, and mass dissemination of ideas, needs this sharpening of the individual will in the shaping of destiny more urgently than ever.

"Man who suffers from the oppression placed upon his will by his upbringing, by society and morality, must relearn to want, to regain his will."[1]

Philosophers like Lewis Mumford in *The Myth and the Machine*, Loren Eiseley in the *Invisible Pyramid*, writing about nature, warn us, unexpectedly, of the need of subjectivity. The need of an axis to permit us to control our orientation in new worlds.

"The myth of the hero always shows a man who wants."[2]

Volonté du Bonheur, this slim and condensed volume, is a guide to this center of interpretation, understanding, evaluations, a center of orientation.

This is the "*Realisierungsprinzip*" which in distinction from the "reality principle" of Freud has a dynamic significance inasmuch as it views reality, not as something given once and for all to which the individual adapts himself more or less, but as something which has come into being, yes, is continuously becoming.[3]

This is a revivifying concept, because we all recognize today the collective neurosis which creates war, and if at an early age we had organically worked for our growth and independence, our happiness and fulfillment, we would not project on to the world our negative and destructive rebellions which come from hopelessness in relation to change, and which causes eruptions to form these vast abscesses we call war.

Unfortunately, happiness was considered a selfish pursuit, and was associated with indifference to the fate of the world.

"The achievement of happiness represents a peak of individualism and its pleasurable will affirmation through personal consciousness . . . "[4]

The disastrous experience of America, with its chaos and confusions, the loss of the self, encouraged by the principle of surrendering the self to the benefit of the community, proved that an unhappy man was more dangerous to society than a happy one. Today we have to recognize that an unthinking mass, easily led by any leader at all, is the most dangerous of all phenomena. It is in America that we witnessed the loss of the self, the loss of the pleasure principle, and the consequent violence. Men, not happy or proud of the work they did, frustrated as human beings, erupted in hostility against man.

Volonté du Bonheur, a small book, the most lucid indicator of this lost self under the pressure of mass media, television, and newspaper, reminds us that an unhappy man is a dangerous man, and that the man who achieves fulfillment radiates an influence of incalculable benefits.

We forgot that negativity is destructive, passivity is destructive, and that reawakening of the creative will which has been subdued and depressed by a sense of guilt which Otto Rank analyzes and dispels can be a more stable foundation for collective well-being.

[1]*L'homme qui souffre de l'oppression qu'exercent sur la volonté la pedagogie, la societé, la morale, doit reapprendre á vouloir.*

[2]*Le mythe des héros montre surtout l'homme qui veut.*

[3]*C'est le principe de réalization qui, différent du principe de réalité (Freud) a une valuer dynamique, parcequ'il ne regarde pas la réalité comme quelque chose de donne une fois pour toutes, á quoi l'individu s'adapte plus ou moins, mais la considére comme un devenir continuel en perpetuelle transformation.*

[4]*Car le desir du bonheur est un point culminant de l'individualisme et son affirmation joyeuse du vouloir par la conscience personelle.*

THE WRITER
AND THE UNCONSCIOUS
From a preface to Anna Kavan's "Ice"

"I HAVE ALWAYS ADMIRED Anna Kavan as one of the few writers who dared to explore the nocturnal worlds of our dreams, fantasies and imagination. It takes more courage and a greater skill in expression. As world events give increasing evidence of the prevalence of irrational impulses it becomes absurd to treat them with rational logic. We have to learn instead how to decipher and understand and then to control the irrational.

◆

"R.D. Laing writes in *Politics of Experience*: `We all live in the hope that authentic meetings between human beings can still occur. Psychotherapy consists in paring away of all that stands between us, the props, masks, roles, lies, defences, anxieties, projections and introjections, in short all the carry-over from the past, transference and countertransference that we use by habit and collusions, wittingly or unwittingly, as our currency of relationship.'

"The writer who exposes the designs and patterns of the unconscious can help us in such revelations. From her very first book Anna Kavan went into this realm, beginning with *The House of Sleep*, a significant beginning; then with a classic equal to the work of Kafka titled *Asylum Piece*. In *Asylum Piece* the non-rational human beings caught in a web of delusions still struggle to maintain a dialogue with those who cannot understand them. To the poet and to the psychologist such symbolic acts and speech are clear and understandable. In later books the waking dreamers no longer try. They face their solitude and tell of their adventures. They reflect faithfully how the world appears and, in this new book, how its absurdities and cruelties can affect a human being.

"We admire deep-sea divers who explore the depth of the ocean. We do not admire enough those who are able to describe their nocturnal experiences, those who demonstrate that the surface does not contain a key to authentic experience, that the truth lies in what we *feel* and not merely in what we *see*. Greater familiarity with *inner* landscapes could in the end illumine the mystery of the human mind. The scientist can *observe* psychological phenomena, but the writer can make us *experience* them emotionally. This book is no mere personal, unique voyage to the antipodes of the mind.

For the unconscious is a universal ocean in which all of us have roots."

Written for the British edition, this preface was never used. It appeared for the first time in ANAÏS: An International Journal, *Volume 9, 1991*

THE MISSION OF THE POET
A preface to the poetry anthology "Rising Tides"

J EAN COCTEAU SAID that poetry was indispensable, but he did not know why. This anthology may answer the question, for every mood, every experience, every aspect of the world, demands expression, and here we might turn casually to any page, and find the words we need for indignation, anger, injustice, love, passion, religious and pagan prayers, cries of distress and cries of joy. We can turn to it on blank days when either our sorrows or our joys do not find their voice. So many poets are gathered here together to voice the entire range of human experience, in every variation of voice and tone, employing every color and every texture, every level of talk, from metamorphosis to plain and homely untransfigured statements.

Poetry is no longer to be defined as of old, it has opened its doors to direct statements, to slogans, to marching songs, to hymns and to street songs. It is no longer a solitary chant, it has become common to all and inclusive of all races, religions and irreligions. The variety of levels and themes makes these poems universal. But it also focuses on revelations of women which needed to be heard. Every age is represented, every race, every individual variation, but ultimately this poetry, this anthology is the song of women.

My own definition of the poet is he who teaches us levitation, because I feel poetry is needed to lift us above despair, and above our human condition, so we may become aware that we need not be overwhelmed by the weight of earth, the ponderous oppression of quotidian burdens. The burdens here are dwelt upon, poetry in this anthology is not only the transformer or the indicator to other forms of life. It is the poetry of today, and the poetry of women at a crucial period of evolution. The selection is wide and broad. It will place poetry as a daily necessity, as a nourishment, as useful to the community, the equivalent of our daily speech, our daily thoughts and feeling. In this way it may prove its indispensable quality. In the terms of Gaston Bachelard, the poet philosopher and philosopher of poetry, we have here the poetics of fire, space, earth, air and water.

Gaston Bachelard writes that "poetry gives us mastery of our tongue." And only by this mastery can we make ourselves understood by others, and make our needs, our demands, our predicaments, our dilemmas, known.

He also writes: "There is no need to have lived through the poet's suffering in order to seize the felicity of speech

offered by the poet—a felicity that dominates tragedy itself."
And: "To transcend too high, or descended too low, is allowed in the case of the poet, who brings earth and sky together."

The poet helps us to see more, to hear more, to discover within ourselves such landscapes, such emotions, such reveries, such relationships to people, to nature, to experience as may remain unknown to us before they describe it, for to sustain our dreams and our lover's needs, we need to absorb from the poet his capacity for seeing and hearing what daily life obscures from us.

Two kinds of space, intimate and outer, struggle for our attention, and struggle for integration, for in integration and fusion lies the power of ecstasy which enables us to conquer despair and conquer human oppression.

Rilke said: "The plain is the sentiment which exalts us." But the description of the not plain is what sustains us in our search, the description of the marvelous states of consciousness attainable is what propels us upward rather than downward.

Poetry, no matter what its subject, can propel us forward, for it gives to man's most ordinary experience, the flow of a tale, the illumination of myth, the song's contagious rhythm, a troubadour's romance.

Gaston Bachelard again: "Any sentiment that exalts us makes our situation in the world smoother."

they sing it, they print it themselves. It is the creative drug, the creative painkiller, the creative tranquilizer, the creative healer.

This is an era of poetry, poetry against the inarticulate, the stuttering, the muttering wordless suffering which cannot be shared or heard. The skillful, the clarified expression of our joys and sorrows, our angers and rebellions, makes them sharable and therefore less destructive. Words as exorcism of pain, indispensable to fraternization, the opposite of war.

The fusion here is in the voice of woman. Woman determined to end woman's mysteries and woman's secrets. We need to know her better. Let us approach her and listen to her in these condensed, in these concentrated and distilled messages, to become intimate with her.

It is not only the Oriental woman who wore veils. There are psychic veils, and these are best lifted by the poet, so we can acquire from the poet at the same time his constant rediscovery of love.

Preface to Rising Tides: 20th Century American Women Poets. *Edited by Laura Chester and Sharon Barba (1973)*

THE ENERGY OF FIRE
A Preface to Marcel Moreau's "Livre Ivre"

T HERE ARE DEPTHS into which most human beings do not dare to descend. These are infernos of our instinctive life, the journey through our nightmares necessary to rebirth. The mythological journey of the hero includes the great battles with our demons. Marcel Moreau is engaged in this battle. At first I thought of him as the Lilauea volcano in Hawaii. Ascending toward its vast pit the trees, flowers, bushes, birds, fruit grew rarer and finally there were none at all. The soft earth had been covered by black lava, not shining as it does when wet and erupting, but the dead color of the blackest ash. It hardened. It burnt trees to bone-white skeletons. Approaching it, it smoked still, ready for other eruptions. It was a vast crater. One could walk to its rim, looking down at the infernal pit. It smelled of sulphur. There was a silence, a suspense, for everyone who leaned over knew what had come before, a wild incredible explosion, fountains of fire, rocks propelled in the air. But in the end, in

Livre Ivre, one does not experience devastation or destruction from Moreau's explosion of fire. He is in search of his humanity, and is dynamiting the obstacles and the injuries which impede his quest. He returns to his childhood. The portrait of his father is deeply moving.

"Tant de pauvres meurent sans donner l'impression d'avoir vecu."

"Sa mort a fait de moi un latteur."

He is suspicious of woman even though:

"Je crois que d'elle seule peut venir l'absolu."

The obstacle to woman was created by the mother. We suffer his schooling, his battles. He exists *sur un pied de guerre.*

"Dans ma famille regnait une sorte de puritanisme sans Dieu."

One feels that if he did not combat he would be possessed by an unfulfillable love and tenderness. Meanwhile his hostility is a kind of passion. In his own beautiful words from a letter to me:

"It is not enough that writing should be a song, it must intoxicate, drug, it must provoke in the reader those sumptuous disturbances without which there are no deep revelations. My wish is to introduce wine in the French language, to write a book which could be danced rather than read."

It is the energy of fire which creates our world. I think of the new earth, lava at first, burning and then cooling and giving birth to the most daring flowers.

His desires are thwarted: he asks for books and is given other objects. He has to struggle not to be submerged by the mother. If his other books were like elemental storms, this one seeks the cause for his furies, his revenges. *"Ce qui m'attriste et me revolte à la fois, c'est d'avoir été le temoin de tant de destinées closes."* Then he discovers the world of the writers.

"Je joue avec ces moments de la vie qui me firent mal, je les integre sans difficultés au chant general d'une démarche qui s'est trempée dans ses profoundeurs en vue de culminer dans l'ivresse." Ecstasy is to be won through the magic power of language. To all the selves in us which are silent, which cannot speak, Moreau gives a tongue. Because he believes that *"chaque homme se doit de devenir le monstre dont il possède en lui, ravages, mutiles, maudits, toutes les composants. En verité mous sommes un puzzle terrible où il n'est aucune piece qui ne soit défigure our distordue par la société. À nous de le reconstituer contre elle, en lui adjoutant les éclairs fabuleux de la nuit."*

By a series of explosions, the poet uncovers what he believes: *"que le souterrain est le royaume de la vie, le repaire de l'ivresse, le bonheur des ombres et des illuminations."*

THE WRITING OF WOMEN

WOMEN HAVE ALWAYS been writers. It was the one profession which did not conflict with the rules imposed on her or the limitations and restrictions of her professional expansion. But this is a dazzling moment for women; it is the moment when the world has become aware of her achievements. For even as writers, women encountered prejudice or at least indifference. At one time they took names of men to be able to assert their work: George Sand, George Elliot. And the election of Colette to the French Academy was bitterly fought on the ground that she merely wrote about love affairs and personal entanglements.

The very restrictions and limitations gave women's writing an added dimension: writing benefited from being at times her only means of expression. She perfected it. In the year 900 a Japanese woman wrote the first chronicle of life at court, the *Tale of Gengi*, equal to a proustian achievement in subtlety of psychology and care for detail.

The writings of women can bear the new intense light of recognition thrown upon it by the woman's liberation movement. It can bear revaluation and critical examination. Women like Anna Balakian and Sharon Spencer have become themselves acute and skillful critics.

The fact that woman was not always involved in larger issues of history or politics increased her vision of deeper issues, those of human values, human concerns, and the value of personal relationship to sustain our humanity endangered by technology and by politician's power drives. History is the story of man's thirst for power with its consequent inhumanity. The writing of women may indicate a new feminine direction. In Yoko Ono's words: "We can evolve rather than revolt, come together rather than claim independence and feel rather than think."

A proper evaluation, a proper perspective and appreciation of women's writing may help to balance the unbalanced forces of the world today. If we have had an excess of violence, of crime and war, we may find in women's writing the persistent devotion to opposite concerns.

From "Feminine Sensibility: A Forum," The Harvard Advocate, *(Winter 1973)*

THE LITTLE GIRL IN YELLOW

S ITTING ALONE at the tennis club (Cercle du Bois), drowsy after a game, I watched the children playing and saw a little girl I wanted to have—an eery child with a secret smile at thoughts of her own, running lightly to dry her hands which she had dipped in the lake.

I must be beaten, I thought sadly, for I am beginning to want to pass my life on to another. Until now I never wanted children. I called them interruptions, renunciations, knowing too well that they might be neither like Hugh nor myself, not even perhaps an extension or a development of our ideals, but a mere repetition of ordinary patterns. . .

Yet this child fascinated me. She drew me out of myself— perhaps that was the blessing. I chased after her fragile self, in yellow, red, left all my weariness far away . . . She was happy to have wet hands, she was happy because the sun was drying them, she was happy to be running. All of a sudden she stood before me, wide-eyed, startled, her arms open, her little yellow dress fluttering. I felt a second of struggle, as if the child were demanding a kind of surrender. And though my body was sore with passion, with hunger, with pain, I smiled, and she liked my smile and ran away, and ran back and around my chair, until her mother called her back.

*Jamais je me donnerais entiérement à rien. . . Jamais je n'échapperais a moi-même, ni par l'amour, ni par la maternité, ni par l'art. Mon "moi" est comme le Dieu des croyants faibles, qui le voient partout, toujours, et ne peuve fuire cette bantise et cette vision.**

I have desired self-perfection and greatness, a very immense conceit—and now I am crushed by the weight of my ambition. I would like to pass the burden to a child.

I will never give myself entirely to anything. . . I will never escape from myself, neither through love, nor motherhood, nor art. My self is like the God of those of little faith, who see him everywhere, always, and cannot flee this obsession and this vision.

From The Early Diary of Anaïs Nin, *Volume IV (July 30, 1929)*

WOMAN OF NEW YORK

T HE CHARACTERISTIC ASPECT of the women of New York is that they are in motion, perpetually active and that one would have to photograph them at a speed used for ballet dancers or athletes. Coming from above, say in a helicopter, we see first on the twenty-fourth floor of one of the highest glass buildings facing the United Nations, Mrs. Millie Johnstone who initiated the first Japanese Tea Ceremony School in New York, to counterbalance its hectic, frenzied activity. Her apartment, one of the most beautiful in New York, is decorated with some of her own tapestries evoking the Bethlehem Steel Works of her husband, with collages by Varda, wool rugs from Peru, and has a view of the Hudson which seems like a view from a transatlantic liner. One room is shuttered by a trellis of wood and frosted glass, subdued and simple. It is a Japanese room, in the style of classical Japanese austerity. A low couch, filtered light, a platform covered by a grass mat for the tea ceremony, the utensils, the pot, the cups, the brush, the spoon, the napkin, the wafer. Mrs. Johnstone dispenses the calm and serenity of the ritual in a blue kimono. Having been a dancer she is very graceful and her New England profile melts into the formal design expected of Oriental stylization. She feels that modern men and women need to learn repose and meditation to sustain themselves in a city of frenzy.

◆

Uptown, in a private house, in an apartment which opens on a backyard as some of the private houses still do in New York, lives a chic, slim, attractive woman, Dr. Inge Bogner. Sitting in a deep, modern plastic black and white chair, knitting, speaking in a soft voice, with lively, keen expression and the most outstanding knowledge of semantics, she wields an influence over the life of New York on two levels, which throw their cumulative power in a widening circle difficult to measure. She treats the neurosis spawned by the city, every day, every hour, creating a circle of sanity, of renewed strength, for New York is like a vast computer, ruthless to human beings. She advises young men in trouble with their draft board, parents who do not know how to be parents, creative people defeated by commercialism, the confused, the discouraged, the lost.

She was born in a small town in Bavaria. Her father was a doctor reputed for his liberalism. Her second activity is in politics, so that her teachings, her psychological insights are not only applied in her office, individually, but she acts out the commitments they point to. Not theory but practice. She has participated in marches, has walked the streets of her neighborhood seeking votes. She is a woman in action, in harmony with her insights.

◆

Xavore Poue is a professional pianist practicing for a concert in a studio in New York. She is a tall and handsome woman. But she is best known as the woman who writes about astrology for *Harper's Bazaar*. The monthly horoscopes are written with imagination and poetry and even when they do not necessarily fit the person one wishes they did. It is a destiny, a life designed by an artist and preferable to reality, for its ambiguity allows for surprises.

On New Year's Eve she is the only one who practices the ritual of putting melted lead into cold water and reading the modern sculpture hieroglyphs as predictions.

She has studied minerals, herbs, health foods, and relates astrology to other knowledge. I would trust her portrait of anyone, for, like the lover, she sees the potential self who might be. She is herself born in the sign of our age so should be able to read its intentions.

◆

Now we travel to the Village, west on notorious Bleeker Street, beyond the cafés and the rock-and-roll nightclubs, where the antique shops begin, arts and crafts boutiques. We are visiting America's greatest writer, Marguerite Young. Art is the nightlife of the people. Marguerite Young is the describer of the American subconscious, just as James Joyce was of his own race. She is totally committed to the pursuit of this oceanic unconscious nightlife. Her apartment is all in red and filled with collections of dolls, angels, tin soldiers, circus horse, mementoes, sea shells, Indian necklaces—a children's paradise. The walls are covered with books. Already celebrated for a classic *Miss MacIntosh, My Darling,* she is modest, continues to teach, eats at drugstores, converses with anyone at all, lives most intensely within the book she is writing so that you are taken into the world she is exploring at the moment, its comic aspects, its anecdotal surprises, its associative infinities. This earthy-looking, plain spoken, middle western American, wafts you into spatial semantic games, elasticities of wildest imagination. For America who only looks at its day action face, this oceanographer of the deep is a phenomenon. When she works the pages cover all her floors, furniture, bookcases, divans, couch, chairs. One day they will fall over the city of New York outshining the paper rain for the astronauts.

◆

In another pink house lives an even more symbolic figure of New York women, for she lives in luxury without serenity, and writes books of poems between telephone calls, hairdressers and dressmakers, frivolities, social activities. She is young and beautiful, graces the pages of *Harper's Bazaar,* is restless, whirling, hectic, paying attention only for sixty sec-

onds, starting a hundred new lives a day, wishing to live in
an orange grove in California, to be back in Hong Kong, or
Cambodia, seeing everyone who has a name, dropping in
on her little girl with her governess while they take air in
the park, saying she cannot write poems all day, so she studies Chinese exercises and writes about them, about sea shells,
is everywhere, knows everyone, never rests anywhere like
a female hummingbird whose hum, the poem, she must
write how and when? One does not know. When she calls
up it is a cry of distress, typical of New York *bas*, for it is
repetitious: New York is a poison (ambition) one cannot believe in friendship. Life is not real (in New York). I am lonely,
everyone admits over the telephone, behind the gusto the
glitter, the metallic surface, the glamor, the activity. The poem
comes out smiling, witty. It is a sport to smile, glide, propelled by what? Who?

From an article, "Fuenf von vier Millionen," in Merian, *a German magazine
published in Hamburg (Number 9/Volume XXIII)*

THE NEW WOMAN

WHY ONE WRITES is a question I can answer easily, having so often asked it of myself. I believe one writes because one has to create a world in which one can live. I could not live in any of the worlds offered to me—the world of my parents, the world of war, the world of politics. I had to create a world of my own, like a climate, a country, an atmosphere in which I could breathe, reign, and recreate myself when destroyed by living. That I believe is the reason for every work of art.

The artist is the only one who knows that the world is a subjective creation, that there is a choice to be made, a selection of elements. It is a materialization, an incarnation of his inner world. Then he hopes to attract others into it. He hopes to impose his particular vision and share it with others. And when the second stage is not reached, the brave artist continues nevertheless. The few moments of communication with the world are worth the pain, for it is a world for others, an inheritance for others, a gift to others in the end.

We also write to heighten our own awareness of life. We write to lure and enchant and console others. We write to serenade our lovers. We write to taste life twice, in the moment and in retrospection. We write, like Proust, to render all of it eternal, and to persuade ourselves that it is eternal. We write to be able to transcend our life, to reach beyond it. We write to teach ourselves to speak with others, to record the journey into the labyrinth. We write to expand our world when we feel strangled, or constricted, or lonely. We write as the birds sing, as the primitives dance their rituals. If you do not breathe through writing, if you do not cry out in writing, or sing in writing, then don't write, because our culture has no use for it. When I don't write, I feel my world shrinking. I feel I am in a prison. I feel I lose my fire and my color. It should be a necessity, as the sea needs to heave, and I call it breathing.

Guilt For Creating

For too many centuries we have been busy being "muses" to the artists. And I know you have followed me in the diary when I wanted to be a muse, and I wanted to be the wife of the artist, but I was really trying to avoid the final issue—that I had to do the job myself. In letters I've received from women, I've found what Rank had described as a guilt for creating. It's a very strange illness, and it doesn't strike men—because the culture has demanded of man that he give his maximum talents. He is encouraged by the culture, to become the great doctor, the great philosopher, the great professor, the great writer. Everything is really planned to push him in that direction. Now this was not asked of women. And in my family, just as in your family probably, I was expected simply to marry, to be a wife, and to raise children. But not all women are gifted for that, and sometimes, as D.H. Lawrence properly said, "We don't need more children in the world, we need hope."

So this is what I set out to do, to adopt all of you. Because Baudelaire told me a long time ago that in each one of us there is a man, a woman, and a child—and the child is always in trouble. The psychologists are always confirming what the poets have said so long ago. You know, even poor, maligned Freud said once, "Everywhere I go, I find a poet has been there before me." So the poet said we have three personalities, and one was the child fantasy which remained in the adult and which, in a way, makes the artist.

When I talk so much of the artist, I don't mean only the one who gave us music, who gave us color, who gave us architecture, who gave us philosophy, who gave us so much and enriched our life. I mean the creative spirit in all its manifestations. Even as a child, when my father and mother were quarreling—my father was a pianist and my mother was a singer—when music time came, everything became peaceful and beautiful. And as children we shared the feeling that music was a magical thing which restored harmony in the family and made life bearable for us.

Now there was a woman in France—and I give her story because it shows how we can turn and metamorphose and use everything to become creative. This was the mother of Utrillo. Because she was very poor, the mother of Utrillo was condemned to be a laundress and a houseworker. But she lived in Montmartre at the time of almost the greatest group of painters that was ever put together, and she became a model for them. As she watched the painters paint, she learned to paint. And she became, herself, a noted painter, Suzanne Valadon. It was the same thing that happened to me when I was modelling at the age of sixteen, because I didn't have any profession and I didn't know how else to earn a living. I learned from the painters the sense of color, which was to train me in observation my whole life.

I learned many things from the artist which I would call creating out of nothing. Varda, for example, taught me that collage is made out of little bits of cloth. He even had me cut a piece of the lining of my coat because he took a liking to the color of it and wanted to incorporate it into a collage. He was making very beautiful celestial gardens and fantasies of every possible dream with just little bits of cloth and glue. Varda is also the one who taught me that if you leave a chair long enough on the beach, it becomes bleached into the most beautiful color imaginable which you could never find with paint.

I learned from Tinguely that he went to junkyards, and he picked out all kinds of bits and pieces of machines and built some machines which turned out to be caricatures of technology. He even built a machine which committed suicide, which I described in a book called *Collages*. I am trying to say that the artist is a magician—that he taught me that no matter where you were put, you can always somehow come out of that place.

Now I was placed somewhere you might imagine would be terribly interesting, a suburb of Paris. But a suburb of Paris can be just as lonely as a suburb of New York or Los Angeles or San Francisco. I was in my twenties and I didn't know anyone at the time, so I turned to my love of writers. I wrote a book, and suddenly I found myself in a Bohemian, artistic, literary writer's world. And that was my bridge. But sometimes, when people say to me, that's fine, but you were gifted for writing, my answer is that there is not always that kind of visible skill.

I know a woman who started with nothing, whom I consider a great heroine. She had not been able to go to high school because her family was very poor and had so many children. The family lived on a farm in Saratoga, but she decided to go to New York City. She began working at

Brentano's and after a little while told them that she wanted to have a bookshop of her own. They laughed at her and said that she was absolutely mad and would never survive the summer. She had $150 saved and she rented a little place that went downstairs in the theater section of New York, and everybody came in the evening after the theater. And today her bookshop is not only the most famous bookshop in New York, the Gotham Book Mart, but it is a place where everybody wants to have bookshop parties. She has visitors from all over the world—Virginia Woolf came to see her when she came to New York, Isak Dinesen, and many more. And no other bookshop in New York had that fascination which came from her, her humanity and friendliness, and the fact that people could stand there and read a book and she wouldn't even notice them. Now Frances Steloff is her name, and I mention her whenever anyone claims that it takes a particular skill to get out of a restricted, limited or impoverished life. Francis is now eighty-six, a beautiful old lady with white hair and perfect skin who has defied age.

It was the principle of creative will that I admired and learned from musicians like Eric Satie, who defied starvation and used his compositions to protect his piano from the dampness of his little room in a suburb of Paris. Even Einstein, who disbelieved Newton's unified field theory, died believing what is being proved now. I give that as an instance of faith, and faith is what I want to talk about. What kept me writing, when for twenty years I was received by complete silence, is that faith in the necessity to be the artist—and no matter what happens even if there is no one listening.

I don't need to speak of Zelda Fitzgerald. I think all of you have thought about Zelda, how she might never have lost her mind if Fitzgerald had not forbidden her to publish her diary. It is well known that Fitzgerald said no, that it could not be published, because he would need it for his own work. This, to me, was the beginning of Zelda's disturbance. She was unable to fulfill herself as a writer, and was overpowered by the reputation of Fitzgerald. But if you read her own book, you will find that in a sense she created a much more original novel than he ever did, one more modern in its effort to use language in an original way.

History, much like the spotlight, has hit whatever it wanted to hit, and very often it missed the woman. We all know about Dylan Thomas. Very few of us know about Caitlin Thomas, who after his death wrote a book which is a poem in itself and sometimes surpasses his own—in strength, in primitive beauty, in a real wake of feeling. But she was so overwhelmed by the talent of Dylan Thomas that she never thought anything of her writing at all until he died.

The Woman of the Future

So we're here to celebrate the source of faith and confidence. I want to give you the secrets of the constant alchemy that we must practice to turn brass into gold, hate into love, destruction into creation—to change the crass daily news into inspiration, and despair into joy. None need misinterpret this as indifference to the state of the world or to the actions by which we can stem the destructiveness of the corrupt system. There is an acknowledgment that as human beings we need nourishment to sustain the life of the spirit, so that we can act in the world, but I don't mean turn away. I mean we must gain our strength and our values from self-growth and self-discovery. Against all odds, against all handicaps, against the chamber of horrors we call history, man has continued to dream and to depict its opposite. That is what we have to do. We do not escape into philosophy, psychology and art—we got there to restore our shattered selves into whole ones.

The woman of the future, who is really being born today, will be a woman completely free of guilt for creating and for her self-development. She will be a woman in harmony with her own strength, not necessarily called masculine, or eccentric, or something unnatural. I imagine she will be very tranquil about her strength and her serenity, a woman who will know how to talk to children and to the men who sometimes fear her. Man has been uneasy about this self-evolution of woman, but he need not be—because, instead of having a dependent, he will have a partner. He will have someone who will not make him feel that every day he has to go into battle against the world to support a wife and child, or a childlike wife. The woman of the future will never try to live vicariously through the man, and urge and push him to despair, to fulfill something that she should really be doing herself. So that is my first image—she is not aggressive, she is serene, she is sure, she is confident, she is able to develop her skills, she is able to ask for space for herself.

I want this quality of the sense of the person, the sense of direct contact with human beings to be preserved by woman, not as something bad, but as something that could make a totally different world where intellectual capacity would be fused with intuition and with a sense of the personal.

Now when I wrote the diary and when I wrote fiction, I was trying to say that we need both intimacy and a deep knowledge of a few human beings. We also need mythology and fiction which is a little further away, and art is always a little further away from the entirely personal world of the woman. But I want to tell you the story of Colette. When her name was suggested for the *Académie Francaise*, which is considered the highest honor given to writers, there was much discussion because she hadn't written about war, she hadn't written about any large event, she had only written about love. They admired her as a writer, as a stylist— she was one of our best stylists—but somehow the personal world of Colette was not supposed to have been very important. And I think it is extremely important because it's the loss of that intimacy and the loss of that person-to-person sense which the woman has developed, because she has been more constricted and less active in the world. So the family was very important, the neighbor was very important, and the friend was very important.

It would be nice if men could share that, too, of course. And they will, on the day they recognize the femininity in themselves, which is what Jung has been trying to tell us. I was asked once how I felt about men who cried, and I said that I loved men who cried, because it showed they had feeling. The day that woman admits what we call her masculine qualities, and man admits his so-called feminine qualities, will mean that we admit we are androgynous, that we have many personalities, many sides to fulfill. A woman can be courageous, can be adventurous, she can be all these things And this new woman who is coming up is very inspiring, very wonderful. And I love her.

From a talk given April 1971 in San Francisco as part of a celebration of women in the arts.

WHAT I WOULD HAVE LIKED TO HAVE BEEN

ETERNALLY A WOMAN of thirty, full-breasted, tall, black hair, Oriental-Spanish eyes and aquiline nose—very pale—exotic looking—extremely experienced—author of five or six books of five or six different kinds (synthetic resume of all interesting attitudes)—unmarried (lovers permitted)—rich enough to help out writers and publish a magazine—a great traveller. At thirty-one I would meet Hugh and have two children (Hugh being the only man I would like to have children from) and sit in an old garden like this one and be really happy.*

*Hugh was her husband and the garden was Louveciennes.

A note written by Anaïs Nin at the age of twenty-seven, at the end of Volume 30 of her original diary, in 1930.